MW01229990

Prescription

Scriptures

Vol. 21 The Power of Prayer

(Pray Without Ceasing)

Written by:

Sunni Barbosa

Prescription

Scriptures

Vol. 21 The Power of Prayer
(Pray Without Ceasing)

ISBN- 9798393459574

Copyright ©2023 by Sunni Barbosa

Published By GODLYGirl Entertainment.

3034 Sterling Rd.

Augusta Georgia 30907

On the corner of Miracle St.

(Referenced from the King James Bible)

Search **Sunni Barbosa** on Amazon.com for more publications.

www.bepurelynatural.com

Please make a small commitment to google GODLYGirl Entertainment and leave us a one-word review, we appreciate your feedback and support!!!

Thank You for Supporting Positive Media!

These

teachings have been inspired by:

Pastor Monique Rice

May she rest in peace as her legacy

lives on.

Speak it into Existence!

Choose the scripture or scriptures that speak life over your situation and recite 3 to 7 times per day to begin manifesting Gods promises over your life today by speaking Gods Word and not your own.

There are no words more powerful than GODs Word's, use them to stab and poke holes in the devil!

Now, doesn't that sound like FUN?

Many of us do not have a clue as to the truly amazing power of Prayer.

For those of us who are so blessed to see the true and living working power of what our prayers to God can really bring.

We hold the power to achieve greatness and the keys to unlock any door.

Prayer can bring life, over death.

Prayer can bring monogamy to a marriage, instead of adultery.

Prayer can mean sobriety, over any addiction.

Prayer can be healing, over any sickness. Prayer can bring unity, over even the greatest of separation.

Prayer can provide peace, in ciaos instantly.

Prayer creates change, to the disfunction that wants to stay the same.

There are some who look to outside sources to give them what they want, but does this really work?

Or does this just stir up God's anger and cause them to be in a worse situation then they were already in.

If they can achieve minor tangible, deceitful results by praying to the devil, fake gods or our ancestors, then image the major results we can achieve by praying to the true one and only most high God, the God of all gods.

The alpha and the omega God.

The possibilities are endless.

Oh, and here's a plus

That I almost forgot to mention, praying to the one and only true and living God helps to ensure that we won't burn in eternal hell fire, how about that…..

What the true God gives to us, the Bible tells us in Proverbs 10:22

He adds no sorrow with it.

Prayer has the power to move things around in the spirt world, just because we do not see it, doesn't mean it's not happening.

When we refuse to pray, we forfeit our power to win against the enemy's attacks.

Once again,

God does not need us to pray,

we need prayer!!!

We need strength,

we need restoration,

we need sanctification.

Prayer is for our benefit and the benefits of others that God would have us to pray for.

God wants our sincere and earnest prayers, prayers that come from our hearts, not just words being repeated over and over again.

As a matter of fact, God does not even need to hear words from our mouths, He wants to hear the words from our hearts.

So be careful what you pray out loud because the enemy can hear, only God knows our deepest thoughts, hopes, dreams and desires.

Prayer is building a relationship with God. Prayer is fighting your battles the right way.

We must learn to pray the correct way, to speak the scriptures of the King James Version Bible that apply to your situation at that present time.

We must not pray aimlessly or speak scripture that do not apply, but instead we must pray with great and powerful intention. Being direct and specific with great belief that out God will harken to our prayers in His son Jesus Christ's Mighty name.

Philippians 4:6-7

Be careful for nothing; but in every thing by
prayer and supplication with thanksgiving
let your requests be made known unto God.
And the peace of God, which passeth all
understanding, shall keep your hearts and
minds through Christ Jesus.

Psalms 18:6

In my distress I called upon the Lord,
and cried unto my God:
he heard my voice out of his temple,
and my cry came before him, even into his
ears.

Matthew 18:20

For where two or three are gathered together in my name, there am I in the midst of them.

Matthew 6:7

But when ye pray, use not vain repetitions, as the heathen do: for they think that they shall be heard for their much speaking.

Romans 12:12

Rejoicing in hope; patient in tribulation;
continuing instant in prayer.

James 5:16

Confess your faults one to another, and pray one for another, that ye may be healed. The effectual fervent prayer of a righteous man availeth much.

Matthew 6:6

But thou, when thou prayest, enter into thy closet, and when thou hast shut thy door, pray to thy Father which is in secret; and thy Father which seeth in secret shall reward thee openly.

1 John 5:15

And if we know that he hear us, whatsoever we ask, we know that we have the petitions that we desired of him.

1 Peter 4:7

But the end of all things is at hand: be ye therefore sober, and watch unto prayer.

James 4:2

Ye lust, and have not: ye kill, and desire to have, and cannot obtain: ye fight and war, yet ye have not, because ye ask not.

Luke 6:27-28

But I say unto you which hear, Love your enemies, do good to them which hate you, Bless them that curse you, and pray for them which despitefully use you.

Acts 1:14

These all continued with one accord in prayer and supplication, with the women, and Mary the mother of Jesus, and with his brethren.

John 15:16

Ye have not chosen me, but I have chosen you, and ordained you, that ye should go and bring forth fruit, and that your fruit should remain: that whatsoever ye shall ask of the Father in my name, he may give it you.

Hebrews 4:16

Let us therefore come boldly unto the throne of grace, that we may obtain mercy, and find grace to help in time of need.

1 Thessalonians 5:16-18

Rejoice evermore. Pray without ceasing. In every thing give thanks: for this is the will of God in Christ Jesus concerning you.

Mark 11:24

Therefore I say unto you, What things soever ye desire, when ye pray, believe that ye receive them, and ye shall have them.

Jeramiah 29:12

Then shall ye call upon me, and ye shall go and pray
unto me, and I will hearken unto you.

Made in the USA
Columbia, SC
10 June 2024